Morey Amsterdam's
BENNY COOKER CROCK BOOK
for Drinkers

Henry Regnery Company • Chicago

Library of Congress Cataloging in Publication Data

Amsterdam, Morey.
  Morey Amsterdam's Benny Cooker crock book for drinkers.
  Includes index.
  1. Cookery (Liquors)   2. Cookery (Wine)   I. Title.
TX726.A34   641.6′2   76-6256
ISBN 0-8092-8138-4

This book is dedicated to my beautiful wife, Kay, our lovely children, Cathy and Greg, and my dear friend and literary agent, Julian Portman.

Copyright © 1977 by Morey Amsterdam
All rights reserved.
Published by Henry Regnery Company
180 North Michigan Avenue, Chicago, Illinois 60601
Manufactured in the United States of America
Library of Congress Catalog Card Number: 76-6256
International Standard Book Number: 0-8092-8138-4

Published simultaneously in Canada by
Beaverbooks
953 Dillingham Road
Pickering, Ontario L1W 1Z7
Canada

Contents

Introduction

The title for this book came from a joke I used to use in my nightclub act. In a routine I did on "being an author," I named *The Benny Cooker Crock Book for Drinkers* as one of my current literary efforts. It always got a big laugh and I thought no more about it until, during a trip abroad, I noticed that in most of the restaurants many of the entrées listed on the menus had some kind of liquor in the "makings." This inspired me to collect recipes—from chefs and other friends all over the world—that had as ingredients beer, wine, or booze.

Such as the following, which is dedicated to Sig Sakowicz:

Hangover Hash

Just eat a plate of your favorite corned beef hash with a poached egg on top. Follow with 2 glasses of tomato juice, a cup of black coffee liberally laced with Polish vodka, and 4 aspirin. Then lie down and sleep it off!

How to Avoid a Hangover

Keep drinking!!

1

Appetizers

****

My uncle was a boozer for thirty years and none of us knew it till one day he came home sober. He and my aunt were engaged for twenty years. She wouldn't marry him when he was drunk and he wouldn't marry her when he was sober.

****

Almond Chicken Tidbits

1 cup cooked chicken, finely ground
¼ pound snappy cheddar cheese spread
Sauterne wine
1 onion, finely chopped
Salt and pepper to taste
1 cup salted almonds, coarsely chopped

Mix together the chicken, cheddar cheese, onion, salt, and pepper. Add enough Sauterne to moisten. The ingredients should hold together. Shape into balls and roll them in the almonds. Yields about 3½ dozen balls.

****

Teetotalers tell you that whiskey has killed more people than bullets. I don't know, but I'd rather be full of whiskey than full of bullets.

****

Cocktail Skewers
(Suggested by Cindy Adams)

1/3 cup Kümmel liqueur
1/3 cup butter
1 package (12 ounces) cocktail franks
20 small mushrooms, washed and drained

In a skillet combine Kümmel and butter. Over medium heat sauté mushrooms and franks in this mixture. Spear one frank and one mushroom on a toothpick. Serve hot. Yields about 20 appetizers.

****

Big papa bear said, "Somebody's been drinking my beer." Mama bear said, "Somebody's been drinking my beer." And the baby bear said, "HIC!"

****

Shrimp-Crab Rolls

¾ **pound cooked shrimp, finely diced**
1½ **pounds crab meat**
1 **onion, finely chopped**
1 **green pepper, seeded and chopped**
1 **hard-boiled egg, chopped**
½ **teaspoon dry mustard**
1 **tablespoon Worcestershire sauce**
1 **tablespoon sweet Marsala wine**
Salt and pepper to taste
Bread crumbs
Olive oil

In a bowl combine the shrimp and crab meat. Add the onion, green pepper, egg, dry mustard, Worcestershire sauce, and Marsala. Salt and pepper to taste. Mix thoroughly and form into bite-sized rolls. Coat with fine bread crumbs and deep fry in olive oil at 370° degrees until lightly brown.

****

"Conductor! Conductor! Lemme off thish train, I thought it was a lunch wagon!"

****

Coquilles Tregaskis

(Named for author Richard Tregaskis)

3-4 tablespoons butter, plus 6 to 8 dabs butter
3 cups mushrooms
4 cups rich cream sauce
½ pound raw lobster tail meat, diced
1 cup frozen oysters, drained, and coarsely chopped
1 cup raw haddock, defrosted, minced
Bread crumbs
Sherry wine to taste

Melt 2 tablespoons butter in a skilled and sauté the mushrooms. Bring sauce to a boil, lower heat, and fold in the seafood and mushrooms. Spoon into six to eight shells or ramekins. Cover with bread crumbs and dot with butter. Wrap in foil and store in the freezer until ready to use. Bake at 350 degrees for about 25 minutes, removing foil wrap for the last 8 to 10 minutes. Pour two teaspoons Sherry over each coquille just before serving. Serves six to eight.

****

Toast to our team: It isn't whether you win or lose . . . it's how you play around!

****

Deep-Fried Mushrooms

Mushrooms
Salt and pepper to taste
Marsala wine
Milk
Egg, slightly beaten
Flour
Bread crumbs
Cooking oil

Remove stems from mushrooms. Salt and pepper undersides and moisten well with Marsala. Let stand one hour. Blot dry. Dip each mushroom in milk, egg, flour, and fine dry bread crumbs. Deep fry at 370 degrees until golden brown.

****

Song Title: Use a Bottle Opener, Grandma, or You'll Ruin Your Gums

****

Avocado-Crab Meat Cocktail a la Sherry

½ cup catsup
¼ cup mayonnaise
¼ cup Sherry
1 teaspoon lemon juice

Dash of cayenne pepper
1 can (6½ ounces) crab meat*
1 cup avocado, diced
½ cup celery, diced

Mix catsup, mayonnaise, Sherry, lemon juice, and cayenne pepper. Beat until well blended. Chill for at least one hour. Shortly before serving, add the crab meat, avocado, and celery. Serves six.

****

A drunk fell out of a second-story window. He lay on the sidewalk, unconscious. When he finally opened his eyes, there was a policeman standing over him asking him what had happened. "I don't know," said the drunk, "I just got here!"

****

Florida Fruit Cocktail

½ cup Port wine
½ cup grape or currant jelly
1 tablespoon lemon juice
Salt to taste
1 cup canned, pitted Royal Anne cherries, drained
1 cup diced canned pineapple, drained
1 cup orange sections, diced

---

*Lobster, shrimp, or tuna may be substituted for, or mixed with, the crab meat.

Simmer wine. Add jelly and stir until melted. Remove from heat. Add lemon juice and salt and let cool. Combine cherries, pineapple, and orange sections in a bowl. Pour wine mixture over fruit. Cover and chill several hours. To serve spoon fruit in cocktail glasses and pour some of the wine mixture over each serving.

****

A drunk in Los Angeles was shaving. He dropped his razor and, just as he bent over to pick it up, a slight earthquake tremor jarred the bathroom and the mirror fell off the wall. The drunk stood up, stared at the blank wall, and screamed, "Oh, my God, I cut my head off!"

****

Janet Gordon's Pastry Appetizers

1 package (9½ ounces) pie crust mix
1 can (2¼ ounces) deviled ham or liver pâté
2 or 3 tablespoons Sauterne wine
Sesame seeds or poppy seeds (optional)

Turn pie crust into mixing bowl. Add deviled ham or liver pâté and wine. Mix gently but thoroughly. Roll out onto a floured board until about ⅛ inch thick. Cut into 2-inch rounds, 4-inch rounds, or 4-by-1-inch strips. Bake on ungreased cookie sheets in hot (450°) oven for 8 to 10 minutes or until lightly browned. Cool before serving. Serve plain or with a favorite spread. Pastries may be sprinkled with sesame seed or poppy seed before baking. Yields 4 to 5 dozen.

****

My uncle hates the sight of whiskey. He says that when he looks at it his mouth waters and he doesn't want to dilute it.

****

Simple Cheese Spread

Blend cream cheese with your favorite cordial. Spread on cocktail bread or rye wafers. Top with a slice of olive, chopped nuts, or tiny shrimp.

****

I knew he was a boozer because he had patriotic eyes—blue with red whites.

****

Anchovy-Wine-Cheese Spread

1 can (2 ounces) anchovies, drained
2 packages (8 ounces) cream cheese
1 cup light Sherry wine
2 tablespoons stuffed green olives, chopped
Pimiento
Green onion for garnish (optional)
Hard-boiled egg for garnish (optional)
Rye bread or crackers

Reserve several whole anchovy strips for garnish and mash the remaining drained anchovies. Soften cheese and blend into mashed anchovies. Beat in Sherry until mixture is smooth. Add olives. Cover and chill for several hours to blend flavors. Serve in a bowl placed in cracked ice. Garnish with strips of anchovy and pimiento topped with a stuffed green olive, finely chopped green onion, or chopped hard-boiled egg. Serve with strips of rye bread or crackers. Yields 1½ cups.

****

The wages of gin is breath!

****

Hot Ham Puffs

1 can (4½ ounces) deviled ham
2 teaspoons dry Marsala wine
1 egg white, beaten
3 tablespoons mayonnaise
1 teaspoon sharp mustard sauce
Bread thins

Mix the deviled ham with the wine. Spread on bread thins. Combine egg white, mayonnaise and mustard sauce and top each puff with this mixture. Brown under the broiler. Serves 12.

****

One of the major film companies was going to make *The Life of Dean Martin* but they couldn't get a liquor license.

****

Fast Liver Pâté

½ pound braunschweiger or smoked liverwurst
½ cup butter
2 teaspoons onion, minced
2 tablespoons chives, finely chopped
2 tablespoons Cognac or Kirsch
Chopped toasted nuts or chopped parsley (optional)

Have the braunschweiger and butter at room temperature. With an electric mixer blend all ingredients thoroughly. Serve as a spread or shape the mixture into a long roll or balls. Dip in nuts or parsley.

****

Doctor: I can't find anything wrong with you, Mr. Jones. It must be due to drinking.
Boozer: Okay, Doc, I'll come back when you're sober.

****

Liverwurst Lovers' Canapés

½ pound liverwurst
1 green pepper, finely chopped
Touch of Tabasco sauce
1 onion, finely chopped
Burgundy wine
Rye or white wafers

Mix together liverwurst, pepper, Tabasco, and onion. Add wine until mixture is the consistency of a spread. Spread on wafers. Yields about 4 dozen canapés.

****

My friend Sam has been drinking for so many years that last month he took a blood test and the doctor offered him sixty dollars a case.

****

Anchovy Appetizer

1 package (8 ounces) cream cheese
2 or more tablespoons Dubonnet Blonde
1 can (2 ounces) anchovies, mashed
1½ teaspoons chopped chives
½ teaspoon Worcestershire sauce
Melba toast rounds

Cream the cheese with Dubonnet. Add anchovies, chives, and Worcestershire sauce. Serve on toast rounds. Yields about 3 dozen.

****

Judge: I hope you understand that you are here for drinking.
Defendant: Okay, Judge. Get the bottle and let's get started!

****

Crab Meat Spread

1 can crab meat or fresh, cooked crab meat
2 tablespoons mayonnaise
½ tablespoon Dubonnet
Pinch of dry mustard
Pinch of ground celery seed
½ tablespoon salt
½ tablespoon chopped olives
1 package potato chips

Flake the crab meat and mix all the ingredients together. Place mixture in a mold and chill. Unmold on a serving platter and surround with potato chips.

****

Husband: Honey, why don't you get our bedroom wallpaper to match my eyes?
Wife: Where am I going to get bloodshot wallpaper?

****

Oyster Snacks with Celery

3 celery stalks, chopped
2 tablespoons butter
2 dozen oysters
1 cup dry Marsala
4 slices toast

Sauté the celery in butter. When tender add the oysters and dry Marsala. Simmer until the oysters' edges curl. Arrange oysters on toast, and pour the remaining liquid over them. Serves four.

****

When a man who doesn't drink gets up in the morning feeling lousy, that's as good as he's going to feel all day.

****

Tuna Spread

1 can (7½ ounces) tuna
½ teaspoon smoked salt
1 or 2 drops Tabasco sauce
1 tablespoon chopped pimiento
1 tablespoon grated onion
1 package (3 ounces) cream cheese
1 tablespoon Dubonnet
2 tablespoons mayonnaise

Flake tuna and add salt, Tabasco, pimiento, and onion. Soften cream cheese with Dubonnet and whip until creamy. Add mayonnaise and stir. Mix the tuna into the sauce and chill. Yields 1½ cups.

****

Accident Report: A big truck carrying cases of Schlitz ran into an ice cream wagon. All over the street—beer a la mode. It was the first time I ever saw a Good Humor with a "head" on it!

****

Ceil Miller's Mushroom-tizer

1 pound mushrooms, finely chopped
2 tablespoons butter
2 hard-cooked eggs, finely chopped
¼ cup Burgundy
1 onion, finely minced
2 tablespoons lemon juice
Garlic salt to taste
White toast squares or crackers

Put all the ingredients in a saucepan and cook slowly, covered, for about 30 minutes. Cool. Spread on toast squares or crackers. Yields about 4 dozen canapés.

****

"You play beautifully. What made you take up the piano?"
"The glass of beer kept falling off my fiddle!"

****

Toni (Mrs. Jan) Murray's Tomato Gobs

13 cherry tomatoes
25 toast rounds
½ cup anchovy butter
4 teaspoons Pernod
25 small cream cheese balls
1 cup mixed nuts, finely chopped
     (do not use peanuts)

Cut cherry tomatoes in half. Spread toast rounds with anchovy butter to which Pernod has been added. Place a tomato half on each buttered toast round and top with cream cheese ball which has been rolled in nuts. Yields 25 canapés.

****

A drunk, weaving his way home, accidentally wandered into a cemetery and fell into an open grave. After lying there unconcious for about half an hour, he opened his eyes, looked around, and muttered, "If I ain't dead, what am I doing here—and if I am, why do I have to pee so badly?"

****

Bourbon-Shrimp Dip

²/₃ cup chili sauce
²/₃ cup catsup
½ teaspoon dry mustard
½ teaspoon salt
1 tablespoon prepared horseradish
¼ teaspoon pepper
3 tablespoons Bourbon
Shrimp, cleaned and cooked

Mix all ingredients together and stir well. Serve with shrimp arranged on cocktail picks. Yields about 1½ cups.

****

Max Bygraves, the famous English comic, told me he thinks that when it comes to mixing drinks, Americans are a little crazy. He said, "First they put in whiskey to make it strong, water to make it weak, lemon to make it sour, sugar to make it sweet. Then they say, 'Here's to you' and drink it themselves!"

****

Wine and Chili Bean Dip

2½ tablespoons butter or margarine, melted
1 can condensed black bean soup
2 tablespoons Dry Sherry
1 teaspoon onion salt
Cheese to taste
Corn chips

In a saucepan combine butter, soup, and Sherry and heat until bubbly. Remove from heat and stir in the cheese. Keep warm over hot water in the top of a double boiler until ready to serve. Serve in a chafing dish over a low flame with corn chips.

****

Did you ever notice that you never see a drunk spill a drink on another drunk!

****

Cheddar Beer Dip

16 ounces cream cheese
1½ cups Beer
16 ounces cheddar cheese, cubed
2 cloves garlic
24 small gherkins

Combine cream cheese and 1¼ cups of Beer in a blender. Cover and blend at high speed for 8 seconds. Add rest of Beer, cheddar cheese, and garlic. Cover and blend again at high speed for 30 seconds or until smooth. Add gherkins and blend 2 to 3 seconds more, or until gherkins are chopped. This will feed plenty.

****

Two drunks were sitting on the beach at Santa Monica, looking out at the ocean.
Drunk: Boy, jes' lookit all that water out there.
Drunker: Yeah, and that's only the top.

****

Dubonnet Dip

1 can (7 ounces) tuna, drained and mashed
3 packages (3 ounces each) cream cheese
¼ cup Dubonnet
1 tablespoon mayonnaise
¼ cup sweet pickle relish, well drained
2 teaspoons parsley, finely chopped
1 teaspoon grated onion
½ teaspoon salt
½ teaspoon garlic salt

Soften cream cheese in Dubonnet, Blend in tuna. Add remaining ingredients and mix well. Cover and refrigerate.

****

A drunk was sitting in a barber's chair with his hat pulled down almost over his eyes.

He said to the barber, "Gimmie a haircut."

The barber said, "You'll have to take your hat off."

"Oh," said the drunk, "I'm sorry. I didn't know the flag was passing by!"

****

Guacamole Dip

2 teaspoons instant minced onions
1/3 cup medium dry Sherry
2 large avocados
4 teaspoons lemon juice
1 teaspoon salt
12 drops of liquid red pepper seasoning
Corn chips

Mix instant minced onions and Sherry. Let stand about 10 minutes. Cut avocados into halves and remove seeds and skins. Mash coarsely (makes about 2 cups of mashed avocado). Combine with Sherry mixture, lemon juice, salt, and liquid red pepper seasoning. Serve with corn chips. Yields about 1 pint.

****

A lady was carrying a duck down the street. Suddenly she was accosted by a drunk who said, "My, what an ugly looking pig!"

She stared at him a moment and replied, "This is a duck!"

He stared back at her and said, "I was talking to the duck!"

****

Sour Cream Dip

1 cup sour cream
1 tablespoon good Bourbon
1 teaspoon finely chopped dill
⅛ teaspoon garlic salt
½ teaspoon lemon juice

Mix together all ingredients. Yields about 1 cup.

****

Wife: (To drunken husband on phone) Where are you?

Drunk: I don't know.

Wife: What do you mean you don't know? Go out and look at the street signs and tell me where you are!

Drunk: Jusht a minute. (Runs out, looks at street signs, and returns to phone.) Hello honey, now I know where I am.

Wife: Well, where are you?

Drunk: I'm on the corner of WALK and DON'T WALK!

****

Whiskey Fruit Dip

¾ cup sour cream
1 tablespoon blended Whiskey, warmed
1 tablespoon light brown sugar

Mix all ingredients and chill. This is great with any fresh fruit, especially berries. Yields about ¾ cup.

****

A car sped down the wrong way of a one-way street, jumped the curb, knocked over a fire hydrant, and finally stopped halfway through the window of a butcher shop.
A cop strolled over and said, "All right, buddy, let me see your driver's license."
"Don't be shilly," said the boozer-at-the-wheel. "Who'd give me a license?"

****

Vi Donahue's Vegetable-Rum Dip

1 cup mayonnaise
1 teaspoon garlic salt
1 teaspoon freshly ground pepper
2 teaspoons light Rum
1 teaspoon chili sauce

½ **head cauliflower, broken into small pieces**
1 box cherry tomatoes
1 bunch green onions
1 bunch radishes
Celery and carrot sticks

Combine mayonnaise, garlic salt, pepper, Rum, and chili sauce and blend well. To serve arrange a platter with the dip surrounded by the raw vegetables. Yields about one cup of dip.

2

Soups

Kay Amsterdam's Apricot Soup

4 cups cold water
1 cup Scotch
½ cup sugar
1 pound dried apricots
3 fresh peaches, peeled and quartered
¼ cup heavy cream
¼ cup tapioca

In a saucepan, combine water, Scotch, and sugar. Add fruit and soak overnight. The next day cook the fruit in the sugared liquid until very soft. Pass fruit and juice through a fine sieve. Heat the soup to the boiling point. Gradually stir in the cream and tapioca and cook, stirring constantly until the soup is thick and creamy. Serve piping hot or chilled.

****

Two drunks wandered into New York's Automat on Broadway. They got ten dollars worth of nickels, dimes, and quarters and walked around sticking them in the food machines until they had their table piled up with salads, sandwiches, hamburgers, steaks, pies, etc. The manager noticed this and started yelling, "You guys are drunk! Get out of here!"

"No, you don't," said one of the boozers. "Not when we're winning!"

****

Black Bean Rum Soup

4 cans (10½ ounces each) condensed black bean
    soup, undiluted
2 cans (10½ ounces each) beef broth, undiluted
½ teaspoon Worcestershire sauce
3½ cups water
1 cup dark Rum
12 lemon slices
Chopped parsley

In a 6-quart saucepan, combine bean soup, beef broth, and Worcestershire sauce. Stir in the water. Bring to a boil over medium heat, stirring occasionally. Reduce heat. Simmer, covered, for 5 minutes. Remove from heat and stir in Rum. Serve at once, garnished with lemon slices and parsley. Serves twelve.

****

"Whatsa matter with you. Ya gettin' snooty or something? Yesterday you wouldn't say 'hello' to me and I saw you twice."
"I never speak to people in that condition."

****

Dee Berman's Party Starter

3 cans (10½ ounces each) condensed beef broth
3 soup cans water
⅓ cup Wine (sauterne, sherry, rosé or burgundy)
Orange or lemon slices, studded with cloves

Combine beef broth and water; add wine. Heat a few minutes to blend flavors. Float clove-studded orange or lemon slices in broth. Guests will appreciate this colorful touch. Yields about eight servings.

****

A man was trying to explain his strange girl friend. He said, "She just won't listen. Everything I tell her goes in one head and out the other. I swear she's got two heads. And she's an awful boozer. One day I bawled her out about her drinking so she hung one head in shame, but with the other she kept right on drinking!"

****

Old English Cheese Soup

¼ **cup dry Sherry**
1 can (11 ounces) cheddar cheese soup
1 cup light cream
½ **cup sour cream**
⅛ **teaspoon celery seed**
1 tablespoon chopped parsley

Blend Sherry and soup in saucepan; stir in light cream. Heat slowly, stirring from time to time. Meanwhile, blend together sour cream, celery seed, and parsley. Garnish each serving of hot soup with a spoonful of sour cream mixture. Yields four to five servings.

****

"Does this bus go to Forty-Seventh Street?"
"Yes, it does."
"Well, g'bye and God blesh you."

****

Cold Gin Soup

Ice cubes
2 cans condensed beef bouillon, or broth
2 cans (12 ounces) vegetable juice cocktail
6 ounces Gin
Pinch of garlic powder or ½ teaspoon garlic salt
Lemon slices

Fill a half-gallon jug with ice cubes. Stir in all ingredients. Serve in old-fashioned glasses. Garnish with lemon slices. Serves eight to ten.

****

Drunk to Hotel Clerk: Gimmie the key to room 307!
Hotel Clerk: I'm sorry, sir, but room 307 is occupied by a Mr. Gordon.
Drunk: I know. I'm Mr. Gordon, I just fell out the window!

****

Lobster-Bourbon Bisque

1 can (10½ ounces) lobster, drained
1 can (10½ ounces) tomato bisque
1 can (10½ ounces) condensed pea soup
3 cups of milk
¼ cup Bourbon

Force lobster through a food mill or blend in an electric blender. In a saucepan combine soups and milk and mix well together. Add lobster and cook over low heat, stirring constantly. Add Bourbon. Mix well. Yields four servings.

****

"Waiter, there's a fly in my soup!"
"I know, our chef used to be a tailor."

****

Kentucky Derby Onion Soup

1 can (10½ ounces) condensed onion soup
⅓ cup Bourbon
1 cup croutons
1 tablespoon grated Parmesan cheese

Prepare soup as directed on label. Heat to the boiling point. Add Bourbon and stir well. Cook and stir over low heat for about 5 minutes. Lightly toss together the croutons and cheese. Pour soup into serving bowls. Top each serving with cheese and croutons mixture. Yields four servings.

****

A drunk, staggering through the park on his way home, stopped in front of the hippopotamus' cage and stared at the hippo, eye to eye, for about ten minutes. Finally, the drunk said pleadingly," Don't look at me like that, honey, I can exshplain everything!"

****

Patty Franklin's Great Onion Soup

5 pounds yellow onions, sliced
¼ pound butter
1½ teaspoons black pepper
2 tablespoons paprika
1 bay leaf
¾ cup flour
9 cans beef bouillon
1 cup any good White Wine
2 teaspoons salt
French bread croutons
Mozzarella cheese, thinly sliced
Parmesan cheese, grated

In a large covered pot, sauté onions in the butter and cook for about ½ hour. Add the pepper, paprika, bay leaf, and flour. Sauté for 10 minutes, then add the bouillon and Wine. Simmer, uncovered, for 1 hour. Serve in oven-proof bowls. Before serving, put a piece of French bread or croutons in the soup and cover with the cheeses. Broil until bubbly. Freezes nicely for future use. Yields six servings.

****

It happened about 10 A.M. in the Bowery in New York City. A gorilla walked into a saloon and sat down at the bar. He ordered a scotch and soda and handed the bartender a ten-dollar bill. It was a little early in the morning for business and the bartender noticed that there was only a twenty-five-cent piece in the cash register. He excused himself and went to a back room to talk to the "Boss." He explained to the Boss that a gorilla ordered a scotch and soda, gave him a ten-dollar bill, and the only change he had in the cash register was twenty-five cents.

"Give him the two-bit piece," said the Boss. He's a gorilla. He won't know the difference."

So, the bartender gave the gorilla the twenty-five cents change. A few minutes later the bartender, feeling a little guilty, looked at the gorilla and said, "You know, we don't get many gorillas in here."

"No wonder," said the gorilla. "How many gorillas can pay nine dollars and seventy-five cents for a scotch and soda?"

****

Oyster Stew

½ pint oysters
2 bay leaves
2 tablespoons butter
½ teaspoon Worcestershire sauce
Salt and pepper to taste
¼ teaspoon paprika
1½ cups milk plus 1½ cups cream (or 3 cups milk)
2 tablespoons dry Marsala wine
Pinch of nutmeg or mace

In a saucepan, place oysters, bay leaves, butter, Worcestershire sauce, salt, pepper, and paprika. Simmer until oysters curl. Discard the bay leaves. Add milk and cream. Simmer again. Add 2 tablespoons of Marsala and top with either nutmeg or mace. Serves two.

****

Cop at the scene of an accident: All right, now. Who was driving this car?
Drunk: Nobody was driving, officer, we were all in the back seat singing.

****

Green Mint-Pea Soup

1 shallot, minced
½ clove garlic, minced
1 teaspoon butter
1 cup chicken broth
Pinch of basil
Pinch of thyme
1 can condensed green pea soup
1½ cups half-and-half
Salt and pepper to taste
2 tablespoons of green Crème de Menthe

Sauté shallot and garlic in butter until soft and golden but not brown. Add chicken broth, basil, and thyme. Bring to a boil and simmer 2 minutes. Blend in pea soup and half-and-half. Add salt and pepper. Strain. Chill for at least 4 hours. Stir in Crème de Menthe. Use more or less, depending on taste. Serves four.

****

It was one of those heavy, pea soup, London fogs. A drunk jumped into a taxi that was parked in front of Claridges. "Take me to Trafalgar Square," he said to the driver.

"You must be off your rocker, mate," said the cabby. "The fog's so thick I can't see two feet ahead of me."

The drunk stepped out of the cab, walked in front of it, and, signaling, yelled to the driver, "Jusht follow me!"

****

Peanut Butter Soup

1 large can of chicken broth
5 tablespoons peanut butter
¼ cup of Sherry

Blend all ingredients together in a saucepan and heat. Salt and pepper to taste.

****

"Say, Charlie, I notice your right arm is much longer than your left arm."
"Thass because my right arm is the one the cops use when they're draggin' me home.

****

Bloody Mary Soup

2 cans (6 ounces each) SNAP-E-TOM
tomato cocktail
1 can (about 46 ounces) tomato juice
1 bay leaf
½ teaspoon garlic
½ teaspoon sugar
5 dashes Worcestershire sauce

40 ounces red madrilène consommé
2 tomatoes, peeled and diced
1 green pepper, diced
½ cup chicken or turkey white meat, diced
5 dashes Tabasco sauce
Salt and pepper to taste
Gin

Bring all ingredients to a boil, then simmer for 10 minutes. Salt and pepper, to taste. Just before serving add ¼ ounce of Gin per serving. Makes about 15 six-ounce cups of soup.

****

Anniversary Toast

My heart said that I needed a wife.
My heart said my life was in a rut.
My heart said I needed a wife.
I wish my heart would keep its big mouth shut!
****

Yau Herbert's Oriental Consommé

1 No. 2 can (20 ounces) tomato juice
1 can (10½ ounces) beef consommé
1 tablespoon butter

¾ **cup Champagne**
Chopped chives, scallion tops, green pepper, celery
    tops, or a combination of these, as garnish

Combine juice and consommé in a saucepan and bring to a boil. Place butter and Champagne in a soup tureen or other serving dish. Pour in boiling mixture and top with a garnish of your choice. Serve immediately. Serves six.

3
Entrées

****

A lady was complaining to her priest about her husband's drinking. "Every night he comes home guzzled to the eyebrows," she said.

"Well," said the good father, "what you've got to do is give him a good scare. That should cure him."

So she went to a costume company and got a Devil's suit. That night she waited in the bushes outside their home for Mr. Booze to come staggering in. Just as he got near the front door, she jumped out of the bushes and screamed, "I AM THE DEVIL!"

"Well," he replied, "shake hands. I married your sister!"

****

Bloody Mary Beef Roulades
(A special recipe from
Edward Robert Brooks, "Gourmet on the Go")

1 can (4 ounces) mushroom pieces
2 tablespoons finely chopped onion

½ **cup crumbled Roquefort cheese, packed**
1 **teaspoon salt**
¼ **teaspoon pepper**
6 **cubed steaks (about 1½ pounds)**
2 **tablespoons flour**
2 **tablespoons butter or margarine**
1¼ **cups tomato-vegetable juice**
¼ **cup Vodka**
1 **tablespoon Worcestershire sauce**
2 **drops Tabasco sauce**
Buttered noodles/rice

Drain mushrooms, reserving juice. Combine mushrooms, onion, ¼ cup of crumbled Roquefort, salt, and pepper. Sprinkle mixture over steaks.

Roll up steaks and fasten securely with toothpicks. Dredge in flour. Heat butter in a large chafing dish or a skillet with a cover. Brown roulades on all sides.

Combine juice from mushrooms, tomato-vegetable juice, Vodka, Worcestershire sauce, and Tabasco. Pour mixture over beef. Cover tightly and simmer for 40 minutes or until tender.

Remove roulades to a heated platter. Stir remaining ¼ cup Roquefort into the pan the roulades were cooked in. Cook, stirring constantly, until sauce is blended. Pour over roulades and serve with buttered noodles or rice. Serves six.

****

A traveling salesman was trying to get a little sleep in his hotel room. Suddenly he heard someone trying to open his door. He jumped out of bed and when he opened the door, there stood a drunk who looked at him and said, "Shcuse me . . . wrong room." Half an hour later, just as the salesman was dozing off, he again heard someone trying to get into his room. He yanked the door open and there stood the same drunk who looked at him and mumbled again, "Shcuse me . . . wrong room." About ten minutes later, it happened again. This time the drunk looked in disbelief at the salesman and asked, "Shay, do you occupy every room in this hotel?

****

Bourbon Stew

(This was invented by a "stew" named Bourbon)

2 pounds lean beef, cubed
2 bottles Red Wine
12 small white onions
8 carrots
3 celery stalks
2 cloves garlic
1 pinch thyme
1 bay leaf
2 tablespoons chopped parsley

3 cloves
1 cup Bourbon
Salt and freshly ground pepper
4 slices bacon, chopped
2 tablespoons flour
½ pound mushrooms, sliced

Make a marinade with one bottle of wine, vegetables, herbs, and cloves. Marinate the beef cubes overnight. Remove the meat to a skillet, coat with the Bourbon, and season with salt and pepper. Discard the marinade reserving the carrots and onions. Heat the skillet, add the bacon, and sauté the meat for 10 minutes, turning until brown. Sprinkle flour over the meat and add the second bottle of wine. Add the carrots and onions (from the marinade), and the sliced mushrooms. Cover and simmer over a low flame for 2 hours, or until the meat is tender. Enjoy! Yields eight servings.

****

Danny Drunk was staggering through the athletic field at his local park when he saw one of the athletes practicing push-ups. He watched the athlete for a few minutes then tapped him on the shoulder and said, "Don't look now, buddy, but I think that somebody stole your girl!"

****

Leatrice Orgel's Chinese Beef

3 scallions, finely chopped
4 tablespoons Chinese oyster beef sauce
4 tablespoons Cream Sherry
2 teaspoons corn starch
1½ pounds flank steak, sliced paper-thin
2 tablespoons cooking oil
Rice

Make a marinade with the scallions, Chinese oyster beef sauce, Cream Sherry, and cornstarch. Add the flank steak and marinate in the refrigerator for several hours before cooking. Over a medium flame heat the cooking oil. Place the marinated meat in the hot oil and stir for about 5 minutes. The meat should be well browned quickly as it is paper-thin. Serve over hot, white rice. (Serves four.)

****

A drunk was leaning up against a lamppost watching the curb go by when a policeman accosted him and yelled, "All right, buddy, let's get moving along. We don't want any drunks in this neighborhood!"

The boozer snarled back at the cop, "Don't give me that 'move along' there, blubber-nose. I live here!"

"If you live here," replied the officer, "why don't you go into your house?"

"Because I forgot my key, wise guy!"

"Why don't you ring the bell?"

"I rang the bell a half hour ago and nobody answered."

"Why don't you ring it again?"

"To hell with 'em, . . . let 'em wait!"

****

Steak au Poivre

4 pounds steak, 1½ inches thick
2 tablespoons whole pepper
Salt to taste
1 teaspoon butter
Celery salt (optional)
2 jiggers Bourbon
1 cup light cream (optional)

Crush the peppercorns with a rolling pin. Place steak on a board and sprinkle half the pepper on each side, patting it with your hand. Sprinkle with salt. Melt the butter in a heavy skillet and sauté the steak. An underdone steak should take 6 or 7 minutes on one side, 4 or 5 minutes on the other. When done the way you like it, remove to a hot plate and season with salt or celery salt.

Add the Bourbon to the pan and mix it well with the pan juices over a low flame. Pour this over the steak. Or, if you prefer a sauce, set the Bourbon aflame and pour it over the steak directly; add a bit more whiskey to the pan, and stir in the cream. Blend and bring to a boil. Serve sauce with the steak. Serves eight.

****

A boozer went to a birthday party and helped the host drink up his presents. At about six o'clock in the morning Mr. Drunk staggered home. He suddenly found himself in front of a house where a party was still going on. He crashed the party, got drunk with a bunch of people he didn't know, passed out, and woke up the next morning in his own bed at home. He had no idea how he got there. All he could remember was that the party was in a house that had a purple door and gold toilet. So he got dressed and started looking for it up one street and down the other. He finally found a house with a purple door, so he rang the doorbell. A lady answers and when she opens the door he asked, "S'cuse me, lady, but does this house have a gold toilet?"

She replied, "Just a minute." Then she turned around and yelled into the house, "Sam here's the guy who threw up in your tuba!"

****

Chili-Wineburger

2 cans (15 ounces each) chili con carne with beans
1 pound ground beef
3 tablespoons fat
²/₃ cup Burgundy wine
2 hamburger buns, halved, toasted, and buttered

Shape beef into 4 flat patties about the size of the hamburger buns. In a skillet heat fat and brown meat well on both sides. In a saucepan bring chili con carne to a boil. Stir in wine. Pour chili mixture over meat, cover, and simmer for 5 minutes. To serve: Place a bun half on each plate and top with meat. Pour chili mixture over all. Serves four.

****

A policeman, finding a drunk lying battered and bruised on the sidewalk, asked the boozer, "Can you describe the man who hit you?"
"Well," said the drunk, "Thash what I was doing when he hit me!"

****

Blended-Glazed Corned Beef

1 corned beef (6 or 7 pounds)
¾ cup blended Whiskey
1 garlic clove
2 bay leaves
4 peppercorns

4 whole cloves
¼ cup orange juice
¾ cup brown sugar
2 tablespoons corned beef stock
1 teaspoon mustard
Rye bread slices (optional)

Place corned beef in a large pot and cover with water. Add ½ cup of the Whiskey, garlic, bay leaves, peppercorns, and cloves. Bring to a boil. Cover and simmer for 3 to 4 hours or until tender.

Remove corned beef and place in a roasting pan. Trim the outer fat and score diagonally in a diamond pattern. Reserve 2 tablespoons of the stock in which the corned beef has simmered.

Prepare glaze by combining orange juice, brown sugar, corned beef stock, mustard, and ¼ cup of the Whiskey in a saucepan. Place over low heat and stir until blended. Pour over corned beef. Bake in a 400° oven for 30 minutes. Keep corned beef warm on a heated tray and slice as needed. Also great when served on rye bread slices, with mustard. Serves ten to twelve.

****

A young mother who had had herself a very wearing day decided that a shot of Scotch would calm her nerves. Right after taking a good stiff drink she put her little girl to bed. As she was kissing the little one good night, the four-year-old looked up and said, "Oh, Mommy, I notice you're using Daddy's perfume."

****

Flambéed Lamb Chops

6 average lamb chops
3 tablespoons onions, finely chopped
¾ cup mushrooms, chopped
¾ cup bread crumbs
3 tablespoons butter
1 teaspoon salt
¼ teaspoon ground pepper
½ teaspoon thyme
1 egg, slightly beaten
½ cup Bourbon
1½ cups cream

Slice into the chops sideways to form pockets for stuffing. Sauté the onion and mushrooms in 2 tablespoons of the butter. Add the breadcrumbs and cook for a few minutes. Take off the heat and mix in salt, ground pepper, thyme, and egg. Stuff this mixture into the pocket you have cut and fasten with toothpicks or skewers.

Brown the chops on both sides in 1 tablespoon butter melted in a heavy pan. Salt and pepper to taste. Add water to cover the bottom of the pan, cover tightly, and simmer over low heat for 1 hour. Turn once in a while.

When tender, pour the Bourbon over the chops and set aflame. Remove the chops. Add cream to the pan, stir well, and heat, but do not boil. Pour over the chops. Serves three or four.

****

Two well-seasoned boozers were sitting at a bar chugging down drinks about as fast as the bartender could come up with them. All of a sudden one of the drunks fell off his stool and passed out. The other drunk gazed at him for a few minutes, then turned to the bartender, and said, "That's what I like about Harry. He knows when he's had enough!"

****

Pork Chops Mexicaine

½ **cup flour**
½ **teaspoon salt**
¼ **teaspoon pepper**
¼ **teaspoon thyme**
6 **pork chops**
3 **tablespoons corn oil**
1 **cup canned peaches**
1 **cup Kahlúa or Coffee Brandy**

Combine flour, salt, pepper, and thyme, and, with a pastry brush, coat both sides of pork chops. Heat corn oil in a frying pan and brown chops. Mix peaches in Kahlúa and pour over chops. Cover pan and cook for 1 hour over a low flame until tender. Serves six.

****

The wife of a friend of ours had purchased a very large grandfather's clock at an antique shop and she sent her husband to pick it up and bring it home. He had the dealer help him strap it on his back. But, as he walked out the door of the antique shop, a drunk staggered into him, knocked him down, and broke the clock into a thousand pieces. My friend was furious. He screamed at the drunk, "Look at what you've done!"

The drunk screamed back, "Wall, why don't you wear a wristwatch like everybody elsh?"

****

Canary Island Roast Pork

5 pounds loin pork roast
¼ cup Coffee Liqueur
2 tablespoons brown sugar
1 teaspoon dry mustard
1 tablespoon guava jelly
Green peas or rice

Preheat oven to 375°. Mix Coffee Liqueur, brown sugar, dry mustard, and guava jelly in a saucepan. Heat until jelly is melted and mixture is bubbly. Brush mixture over entire roast and place in the preheated oven for about 2 hours, or until well done. Baste with sauce every half hour. Serve on a bed of green peas or rice, or both. Serves six or eight.

****

Student: Hy'a Coach.

Prof: Don't you know you're not supposed to drink while you're in training?

Student: What maksh you think that I've been drinking?

Prof: Because I'm not the coach!

****

Potée à la Boulangère

1½ pounds boneless lamb shoulder, cut in large cubes
1½ pounds boneless pork shoulder, cut in large cubes
1½ pounds beef chuck, cut in large cubes
1 cup chopped onions
2 cloves chopped garlic
1 bay leaf
2 cloves
Sprig of thyme
2 large, sliced carrots
1½ cups White Wine
Salt and pepper to taste
2 pounds potatoes, sliced
Beef stock

Put cubed meats into a deep earthenware or enameled bowl with the onion, garlic, bay leaf, cloves, thyme, carrots, and Wine. Season with salt and pepper to taste. Marinate for 8 hours, turning occasionally.

Line a 6-quart casserole with half the potatoes, put meat on top, and pour marinade over the top. Cover with the remaining potatoes and add enough beef stock to come almost to the top of the potatoes. Cover casserole and make the lid airtight by sealing with a flour and water paste. Cook in 325° oven for 3 hours. Serves eight.

****

Two drunks were walking along a railroad track. After about half an hour one of them said, "Ain't this the longest stairway you've ever seen?"

The other one replied, "It ain't the stairs that bother me, it's these low banisters!"

****

Beer-Veal

(Cutlets with a "head" on 'em!)

12 slices Italian veal cutlet
12 slices boiled ham
3 sweet pickles, cut into four strips each
Salt and pepper to taste
2 tablespoons butter or margarine
2 tablespoons corn oil

½ **cup chicken broth**
1 cup Beer
1 cup sour cream
2 tablespoons drained capers
Noodles
Parsley and radishes as garnish

Pound veal cutlets until thin. Put ham slices on top of veal, trimming ham the same size as the cutlets. Top with strips of pickle and roll up to enclose the pickle. Fasten with toothpicks. Sprinkle veal with salt and pepper.

Heat butter and oil in a large skillet and brown veal on all sides. Add broth and Beer. Cover tightly and simmer for 30 minutes or until veal is tender. Remove and keep warm.

Stir sour cream and capers into the pan drippings. Reheat but do not boil. Put veal on top of hot cooked noodles and spoon caper-beer sauce over them. Garnish with parsley and radish rose. Serves six.

****

"Honey, I can't find my glasses."
"Why don't you look where you emptied them last night?"

****

Tony Romano's Veal Scallopini

3 pounds veal, thinly sliced
2 eggs, slightly beaten
1½ cups dry bread crumbs
Oil and butter, as needed
1 pint mushroom-tomato sauce
Sherry wine

Dip slices of veal in beaten eggs, then in bread crumbs. Chill about ten minutes. Sauté veal in equal parts of oil and butter until golden on each side. Place slices overlapped in a shallow casserole. Add mushroom-tomato sauce laced with Sherry. Bake 20 minutes. Serves twelve.

****

"I will now play the *Hungarian Rhapsody* by Goulash."
"Goulash is a stew."
"I don't care how much he drinks. He writes good music!"

****

Veal Venutti Rolino

12 thin slices veal
12 slices mozzarella cheese
12 slices prosciutto

½ **cup butter**
½ **cup dry Marsala wine**
½ **teaspoon salt**
¼ **teaspoon pepper**

Pound veal slices until flat. Place one slice of mozzarella and one slice of prosciutto on each cutlet. Roll together loosely, fastening each cutlet with a toothpick. In a skillet melt the butter and brown the veal on all sides. Lower heat and cook until tender. Remove meat from pan and pour in the Wine. Scrape pan, add salt and pepper, and simmer for 1 minute. Pour sauce over Rolino. Serves four.

****

A drunk was lost in the frozen wastes of Alaska. Two days had passed and he thought he was done for. Suddenly he saw approaching him a huge Saint Bernard dog with a small barrel of whiskey hanging under his neck. "Thank God," he yelled. "At last, man's best friend attached to a dog!"

****

Chicken au Grand Marnier

1 disjointed frying chicken, 2½ to 3 pounds
½ **cup orange sections**
½ **cup Grand Marnier**
6 tablespoons brown sugar
1½ cups large sliced frozen peaches
2 tablespoons vinegar
1 teaspoon nutmeg
1 teaspoon basil

1 clove chopped garlic
½ cup flour
1 teaspoon salt
1 teaspoon pepper
½ tablespoon vegetable shortening

Combine in a saucepan orange sections, Grand Marnier, sugar, peaches, vinegar, nutmeg, basil, and garlic. Cook slowly for about 10 minutes.

Meanwhile roll chicken in flour seasoned with salt and pepper, and brown in vegetable shortening in a heavy skillet. Remove chicken from skillet. Pour off the shortening retaining the residue in the bottom.

Return chicken to the skillet and add contents of saucepan. Cover and simmer about 25 minutes. Serves four.

****

The distraught wife of a longtime boozer finally sought help from her priest.

"It's terrible, Father," she complained. "Every night he comes home stewed to the gills. I yell at him, I scream at him, but it doesn't do any good."

"You're using the wrong approach," said the good priest. "Try kindness. Be affectionate and warm and I'm sure he"ll change his ways."

"I'll try it," she said. So that night when her "old man" came home roaring drunk, instead of berating him, she greeted him with great affection and a few hugs and kisses. She even gave him a short shot of his favorite Scotch. "And now," she whispered, "would you like to go to bed?"

"Might as well," he answered. "I'll get hell when I get home, anyway!"

****

Drumsticks and Spaghetti
(Suggested by Earl "Mad Man" Muntz)

1 package (8 ounces) spaghetti
6 large drumsticks
Salt and pepper
¼ cup melted butter
1 can (1 pound) stewed tomatoes
1 can (6 ounces) tomato paste
1 cup Beer
1 clove garlic, minced
¼ cup grated Parmesan cheese

Cook spaghetti according to the package directions until tender but firm. Drain and rinse with hot water. Put spaghetti into a well-greased, shallow casserole. Sprinkle drumsticks with salt and pepper. Heat butter in a skillet and brown drumsticks on all sides. Place drumsticks on spaghetti. Combine remaining ingredients except cheese and pour over casserole. Sprinkle with cheese. Bake in a preheated moderate oven (350°) for 45 to 50 minutes or until chicken is brown and tender. Serves three or four.

****

Our grand piano is so old only half the keys are left. When you play "Cocktails for Two," it comes out, "Short Beer for One."

****

Lemon-Whiskey Chicken

1 broiler-fryer (3 pounds), cut into serving pieces
Juice of one lemon
3 slices bacon
¼ pound butter
3 shallots, finely minced
½ teaspoon salt
6 grinds fresh pepper
½ cup sifted flour
½ cup Blended Whiskey
½ teaspoon sugar
½ cup dry, White Wine or Dry Vermouth
1 cup mushrooms, sliced
2 egg yolks
½ cup chicken stock
½ cup heavy cream
2 tablespoons strained, fresh lemon juice
Salt and pepper
Parsley for garnish

Marinate chicken pieces in lemon juice for 1 hour. Blanch bacon by dropping into boiling water for 1 minute. Dry.

Melt butter in a large skillet over medium heat. Sauté shallots in butter for about 3 minutes until limp, stirring constantly to prevent burning.

Remove the chicken from the marinade. Add salt and pepper to flour and sift onto a plate or foil wrap. Dust each piece of chicken with seasoned flour and sauté in the same skillet with the shallots and butter until golden on both sides.

Warm the Whiskey in a small pan and pour over the chicken. Set it aflame. When flames ebb, add the lemon juice, bacon, sugar, White Wine, and mushrooms. Cover and simmer for an hour or until chicken is tender and juices run clear. Keep warm while preparing the sauce.

Beat egg yolks in a small bowl until lemon colored. Warm chicken stock but do not boil. Very slowly add stock to beaten eggs, beating briskly. Warm the heavy cream and add to egg yolk mixture, beating briskly. Add lemon juice, salt, and pepper. Pour sauce into a small saucepan and, over low heat, cook until slightly thickened, no more than 5 or 6 minutes. Sauce should be thin but able to coat a spoon. Arrange chicken on a heated oval platter. Pour sauce over and garnish with chopped parsley. Serve with boiled new potatoes and a large tossed green salad. Serves four to six.

****

Old Poem: There's the love of a man for a woman
And the love of a babe for its mother
But the strongest, closest love of all
Is the love of one dead drunk for another!

****

Murray Silverman's Scotch Chicken

4 breast frying chickens with ribs attached
4 tablespoons grated Parmesan cheese
4 tablespoons sharp cheddar cheese
1 cup mayonnaise
3 teaspoons dry mustard
1 tablespoon coarse pepper
Handful of ground walnuts
4 tablespoons Scotch
Salt (optional)

Combine cheeses, mayonnaise, dry mustard, pepper, and Scotch. Place chicken in a well-greased shallow baking pan. Spread mixture thickly over chicken breast. Sprinkle ground walnuts on top of chicken. Cover and bake at 425° for about 45 minutes.

Uncover, baste, and place under broiler to brown, if desired. Serve on a bed of brown rice and use remaining pan fluids as additional gravy. Serves four.

****

Toast: Here's to you, my dearest one
I know your love is true
But if you ever decide to cheat
Tell me and I'll cheat, too!

****

Cheese n' Wine Chicken
(By Rosemarie)

3 pounds chicken
1 can cream of mushroom soup
1 can (2½ ounces) sliced mushrooms
1 clove garlic (or more, according to taste)
Pepper
Garlic salt
1 cup of White Wine
1 teaspoon curry powder
½ pound sharp cheddar cheese
Paprika

Place chicken in open roaster. In a large bowl, mix together mushroom soup, sliced mushrooms, garlic, pepper, garlic salt, and curry powder. Add wine, mix, and pour over chicken. Grate cheese and sprinkle lavishly with paprika. Roast chicken in a 325° oven for 2 hours. This dish can be prepared a couple of hours before serving. Serves four.

****

It was Eli Whitney who said, "Keep your cotton-pickin' hands offa my gin!"

****

Georgia Duckling

1 duckling, 4 to 6 pounds
1 orange, quartered
1 clove garlic
1 teaspoon salt
¼ cup melted butter or margarine
½ cup Bourbon
½ cup orange marmalade

Preheat oven to 425°. Fill duckling cavity with orange quarters, garlic, and salt. Close cavity with small skewers or toothpicks. Lace with twine and truss. Place duckling on rack in a shallow roasting pan; brush with butter and marmalade. Pour Bourbon over duckling and roast uncovered for 30 minutes. Serves two or three.

****

A drunk, watching a revolving door, saw a man walk in. A few seconds later a pretty girl stepped out. "It's a good trick," he said, "but I still don't know what she did with the guy's clothes!"

****

Smoked Almond Turkey Chinese Style

2 to 4 tablespoons cooking oil
2 cups cooked turkey, diced
½ cup water chestnuts, diced
½ cup bamboo shoots, diced
½ cup celery, diced
½ cup mushrooms, sliced
2 tablespoons Sherry
½ cup turkey broth
½ tablespoon sugar
Salt and pepper to taste
Monosodium glutamate (MSG) to taste
½ cup snow peas
2 teaspoons cornstarch
Smoked almonds
Rice

Heat oil in a skillet. Add turkey and brown lightly. Remove turkey and set aside. Add water chestnuts, bamboo shoots, celery, and mushrooms to the oil and cook until the vegetables are tender but crisp. Add Sherry and broth reserved from cooking turkey. Cover and steam less than a minute. Add sugar, salt, pepper, and MSG to taste. Add peas and cooked turkey. Blend cornstarch with a little cold water to make a smooth paste and slowly add. Cook and stir until thickened. Sprinkle generously with almond halves and serve with fluffy hot rice. Serves four.

****

Navy Toast: Here's to the mighty ships we sail
through all those storms and fogs.
And here's to the Dramamine we take
or we'd all be sick as dogs!

****

Rosemarie (Mrs. Danny) Thomas' Baked Halibut in Shrimp-Wine Sauce

1½ pounds halibut steak, cut ¾ inch thick
¾ cup flour
1 teaspoon salt
½ teaspoon paprika
1 can frozen condensed cream of shrimp soup, defrosted
¾ cup dry Sherry
¾ cup water

Coat halibut steak with a mixture of flour, salt, and paprika. Place in a well-greased baking dish. Combine soup, wine, and water and pour around fish. Bake at 400° for 20 to 25 minutes or until fish flakes easily. Makes four to five servings.

****

A lady was sitting in the parlor car, holding her baby on her lap. Across the aisle a drunk kept looking at the child and finally exclaimed, "Lady, that's the ugliest baby I've ever sheen." The lady was furious. She called for the conductor and had the drunk thrown off the train. Trying to apologize to the lady for the rudeness of the drunk, the conductor said consolingly, "I'm so sorry, madam. We wouldn't have you insulted like this for anything. Is there something I can do to make you feel better? Can I get a banana for your monkey?"

****

Crabmeat Jacobs

(Suggested by June Jacobs)

8 green onions, chopped
1 green pepper, chopped
¼ pound butter
1 pound cooked crabmeat
½ cup dry White Wine
½ cup Cognac
Salt and pepper to taste
Tarragon to taste
Chopped parsley
4 slices toast

Sauté the green onions and green pepper in butter. Add crabmeat, White Wine, and season with salt, pepper, and tarragon. When crabmeat is heated, add chopped parsley and warm. Ignite Cognac and add to crabmeat. Serve on toast. Serves four.

****

The wife of the town-drunkard was thoroughly disgusted with him coming home guzzled to the eyebrows every night. She decided to teach him a lesson. At three o'clock one morning, she "poured" him into the back of the family car and took him to a local distillery. The late shift was busy distilling, bottling, and labeling hundreds of bottles of whiskey. "There," she screamed. "Take a look at all those cases of booze! No matter how hard you try, you couldn't drink up all that stuff!" "I know," replied the drunk, "but as you see, I've got 'em working nights!"

****

Drunken Lobster
(By John Flores)

1½ pounds lobster tails
½ cup lobster stock
2 tablespoons butter
2 shallots, finely chopped
3 green onions, chopped
½ cup tomatoes, chopped
2 teaspoons Pernod
½ cup sour cream
1 tablespoon Tequila, warmed for flaming
2 teaspoons chopped chives
Rice

Put lobster in a pot and add enough water to cover. Bring to a boil. Reduce heat and simmer about 5 minutes. Remove lobster and let cool. Reserve one-half cup of the lobster stock. Remove shell and cut meat into slices. Complete the remaining steps at the table. Heat butter in a pan or chafing dish. Sauté shallots and onions until soft. Add chopped tomatoes and blend well. Add lobster slices and Pernod and cook and stir about 2 minutes. Now stir in lobster stock and sour cream very slowly. Heat through. Lightly warm Tequila in a spoon and pour over lobster. Garnish with chives and serve immediately with rice. Serves four.

****

"My uncle stopped drinking because he got an awful scare."
"What scared him?"
"One day when he was shaving, he accidentally cut himself and he lost so much blood his eyes cleared up!"

****

Lobster Salad

1½ pounds fresh, cold lobster
3 cups mushrooms, cooked, chilled, and sliced
¼ cup Grand Marnier
½ cup mayonnaise
Juice of ½ orange
Juice of ½ lemon

2 tablespoons catsup
½ teaspoon Dijon mustard
¼ teaspoon English mustard
1 teaspoon salt
1 teaspoon pepper
Lettuce leaves

Combine lobster meat and mushrooms in a bowl. Blend together the remaining ingredients except the lettuce for the dressing. Pour over the lobster and mushrooms and toss until well mixed. Serve on a bed of lettuce. Serves four.

****

They say that booze and gasoline don't mix. They do, but they taste lousy.

****

Shrimp and Artichoke Casserole

1 can (14 ounces) drained artichoke hearts
1 pound cleaned, cooked shrimp
¼ pound mushrooms
2 tablespoons butter
1½ cups medium white sauce
1 tablespoon Worcestershire sauce
¼ cup dry Sherry
¼ cup grated Parmesan cheese
Salt and pepper to taste
Paprika to taste
Fresh parsley as garnish

Arrange drained artichoke hearts in a buttered casserole; spread shrimp over top. Sauté the mushrooms in the butter until golden. Place on top of shrimp. Prepare a medium white sauce; add Worcestershire sauce and dry Sherry and blend together. Pour over the shrimp mixture. Sprinkle Parmesan cheese over all. Season with salt, pepper and paprika. Bake in a 375° oven for 35 minutes or until brown and bubbly. Serve hot, garnished with fresh parsley. Serves four.

****

Shoestring Cocktail: Two drinks and you're fit to be tied.
Jack Horner Cocktail: One drink and you lay in the corner all night.
David and Goliath Cocktail: A small one and you're stoned.
Hangman's Cocktail: Two drinks and you start swingin'!

****

Shrimp Shanghai

2 pounds shrimp, shelled and deveined
½ cup soy sauce
½ cup Rye Whiskey
¼ teaspoon powdered ginger
1 clove garlic, finely minced
1 teaspoon sugar
½ cup chicken stock

4 tablespoons vegetable oil
1 cup green peas
8 water chestnuts, sliced
2 teaspoons cornstarch
Rice
Cherry tomatoes

In a large bowl make a marinade of soy sauce, Rye, ginger, garlic, sugar, and chicken stock. Marinate shrimp for 1 hour. In a wok or a large skillet heat the oil over a high flame. Drain shrimp reserving marinade. Fry the shrimp in the hot oil, stirring constantly, for 2 to 3 minutes. Add peas and fry 1 minute, stirring. Add water chestnuts and fry 1 minute more. Remove shrimp to a hot platter and keep warm. Mix cornstarch with a small amount of water to make a thin paste; add to the marinade. Pour marinade into the skillet with the peas and water chestnuts and stir continuously for 3 to 4 minutes or until sauce has thickened and become glossy. Pour over shrimp and serve at once with hot steamed rice and tiny cherry tomatoes. Serves four.

****

In the days of the Old West a "tenderfoot" was standing at a bar having a beer when a rough-looking cowboy walked up to the bartender and said, "Gimmie a strychnine cocktail—lots of iodine, two drops of arsenic, and a jigger of rum."

"My," said the tenderfoot, "they sure must be plenty tough where you come from."

"You can say that again," said the cowpoke. "They threw me out for being a fairy!"

****

Tight Tuna Louis

2 cans (7 ounces each) flaked tuna
1 cup diced celery
Shredded lettuce
²/₃ cup mayonnaise
¹/₃ cup chili sauce
3 tablespoons dry Sherry
3 tablespoons chopped ripe olives
Tomato wedges
2 hard-boiled eggs, sliced

Mix tuna and celery and place on a bed of lettuce. Cover with a dressing made of mayonnaise, chili sauce, Sherry and olives. Garnish with tomato wedges and egg slices. Serves four.

****

A drunk was leaning against a lamppost watching the curb go by. He looked up to see a car barreling down the street. It raced by him, jumped the curb, and ran into the side of a building. The drunk ran over to the car and noticed a priest sitting behind the wheel. "Are you all right, father?" he asked.

The priest replied, "I'm fine, son, thank you. I'm really not hurt. God was riding with me."

"Wow," said the drunk. "He better get a new chauffeur. You're gonna get Him killed!"

****

Scrambled Eggs with Brandy

4 to 6 eggs
½ cup canned lobster bisque
2 tablespoons diced lobster meat
¾ cup heavy cream
2 teaspoons Brandy
2 tablespoons butter
Salt and pepper to taste

Beat the eggs with a wire whisk. Combine the lobster soup and meat, cream, and Brandy. Stir into the eggs. In a skillet melt the butter. Pour in the egg mixture and scramble.

****

Benny the Boozer ran into a bar, rushed over to the bartender, and shouted, "Gimme a drink, quick, before the trouble starts!" The excited bartender poured him a whiskey. Benny downed it immediately, then exclaimed, "One more drink, quick, before the trouble starts!" Again the bartender obliged; Benny downed it, and cried out again, "I gotta have one more before the trouble starts!" The bartender eyed him skeptically and asked, "Before *what* trouble starts?"

Without blinking an eye Benny replied, "The trouble thats gonna start now 'cause I can't pay for my drinks!"

****

Clam Omelette

2 cans (7 ounces each) minced clams
2 sticks butter
3 tablespoons flour
²/₃ cup clam juice
½ cup heavy cream
½ pound mushrooms finely chopped
1 teaspoon finely chopped fresh dill
¹/₃ cup Cognac or Zubrowska (Polish Vodka)
Salt and freshly ground black pepper, to taste
15-20 eggs
6-8 teaspoons water
6-8 pinches of salt
2 tablespoons chopped parsley

Drain the clams and reserve ²/₃ cup of the clam juice. Prepare a rich cream sauce by melting 3 tablespoons of butter in a saucepan; add the flour, clam juice, and heavy cream. Stir over low heat until the sauce is thickened. Sauté the mushrooms in 5 tablespoons butter. To the sauce add the clams, mushrooms, dill, and Cognac or Zubrowska. Simmer for 5 minutes. Salt and pepper to taste.

Allow about 2½ eggs per omelette, adding 1 teaspoon of water and a pinch of salt to each. For each omelette beat eggs, water, and salt together. Heat 1 tablespoon butter in an omelette pan and add egg mixture. Prepare omelette in the usual way. If necessary, consult a standard cook-book. Fill each with spoonfuls of clam sauce. Garnish with chopped parsley. Serves six to eight.

****

We've all heard stories about the hardy people of the Old West. For instance, one day a man, his wife, and small son walked into a saloon. "Give us two whiskeys," said the man. "Wassa matter, Pop?" asked the kid. "Ain't Maw drinkin?"

****

Hong Kong Almond Soufflé

Butter for greasing
Sugar for dusting
2 tablespoons cornstarch
2 cups milk
8 eggs, separated
1 cup sugar
¼ teaspoon salt
1 teaspoon almond extract
1 teaspoon vanilla extract
¼ cup ground almonds
2 tablespoons Almond Liquor
Mandarin Sauce (recipe follows)

Butter a 2-quart soufflé dish and dust it with sugar. Put cornstarch in a saucepan and slowly add milk, stirring until smooth. Bring to a boil over medium heat, stirring frequently, and boil 1 minute. Combine egg yolks, ¾ cup sugar, and salt and beat until thick and light. Slowly pour in milk mixture, stirring briskly. Cool 10 to 15 minutes. Add almond extract and vanilla extract. Beat egg whites until soft peaks form. Gradually add remaining sugar and continue to beat until stiff, glossy peaks form. Fold gently into egg yolk mixture. Pour into prepared soufflé dish. Set soufflé dish in a shallow pan filled with 1 inch of hot water. Sprinkle the top of the soufflé with ground almonds. Bake in a 325° oven for about one hour. Serve with Mandarin Sauce. Serves six.

****

Mandarin Sauce

1 tablespoon butter
1 tablespoon cornstarch
½ cup sugar
¼ teaspoon salt
1½ cups tangerine juice
2 tablespoons grated tangerine zest
2 tangerines, peeled and sectioned
2 tablespoons Apricot Brandy

Melt butter in a heavy saucepan. Stir in cornstarch, sugar, and salt. Slowly add the tangerine juice and stir until smooth. Keep stirring over medium heat until sauce boils, is clear, and has thickened. Add tangerine zest, tangerine sections, and Apricot Brandy and stir until blended. Serve warm with Hong Kong Almond Soufflé (preceding recipe) or with ice cream. Makes about 1½ cups.

****

Old Scotch Toast
A friendly lass and a friendly glass
Go very well together;
But of a friendly lass and a friendly ass,
I think a damned sight better;
So here's to the lass and the glass and the ass
May they meet in all kinds of weather;
And we'll drink of the glass and feel of the ass
and make the lass feel better!

****

Nina Rosenberg's Fine Fondue

½ **pound Swiss cheese**
½ **pound Gruyère cheese**
3 tablespoons flour
1 clove garlic
2 cups Riesling or Neuchâtel White Wine
4 tablespoons Gin
1 grind pepper
1 pinch nutmeg
French bread cubes

Cut both cheeses into small cubes. Toss with the flour. Rub a heavy rounded saucepan with a cut clove of garlic and discard. Pour in 2 cups of dry, White Wine. Heat until bubbles rise but *do not* boil. Add a handful of cheese at a time while stirring constantly in a figure-eight motion. When cheese is melted add the Gin, pepper, and nutmeg. Stir until blended. Keep hot over a very low flame, stirring occasionally. Spear bread cubes onto fondue forks and dunk and swirl in the fondue. Serves four.

****

"Why do you drink so much?"
"I drink to forget."
"Forget what?"
"I forgot!"

****

Bob Cosden's Welsh Rarebit

1 cup Beer
1 tablespoon butter
1 pound cheddar or American cheese
2 egg yolks
2 ounces milk
Worcestershire sauce to taste
Toast wedges

Pour Beer into a chafing dish or double boiler and add butter. Warm over low heat and add cheese. Allow to melt slowly, stirring until smooth. Mix egg yolks, milk, and Worcestershire sauce together and blend into cheese mixture. Serve on toast wedges. Serves three to four.

****

A devout drunk walked into his church and said to the priest, "Father, I've come for confession."
The priest said, "Son, I'm very busy tonight so if it isn't something serious like murder, please come back tomorrow night."
The drunk agreed and as he was walking out of the church he ran into another drunk. "Where ya going?" he asked.
The other drunk said, "I'm going to confession."
"Wall," said the first drunk, "come back tomorrow night. Tonight he's only handling murders!"

****

Tequila Barbecue Sauce

1 cup catsup
¹/₃ cup Tequila
Few drops Tabasco sauce
¼ cup molasses
¼ cup vinegar
1 tablespoon Worcestershire sauce
2 teaspoons soy sauce
½ teaspoon dry mustard
¼ teaspoon pepper
2 cloves crushed garlic
1 tablespoon lemon juice

Mix all ingredients well together. Let stand for several hours. Use as a marinade or basting sauce for hamburgers, frankfurters, spareribs and other meats. Makes about 2 cups.

4

Vegetables

****

Doctor to old boozer: After examining you I find that the only thing that will cure your deafness is if you cut out women and liquor.

Boozer to old doctor: What . . . just to hear a little better?

****

Polish Asparagus

2 jars canned asparagus
Salt and freshly ground black pepper, to taste
2 tablespoons Bourbon
1 hard-boiled egg, finely chopped
¼ cup parsley, minced
3 ounces sweet butter
3 tablespoons bread crumbs

Heat asparagus in a saucepan. Arrange on a hot serving platter with the tips going in one direction. Sprinkle tips with salt and pepper and 1 tablespoon of the Bourbon. In alternate layers sprinkle hard-boiled egg and parsley across the tips. Melt the sweet butter and sauté very fine bread crumbs until lightly browned. Pour over asparagus and dribble the other tablespoon of Bourbon over whole dish. Serve very hot. Serves four.

****

A drunk on a bus was staring at a lady across the aisle. Finally he said. "You know something, lady, you are the ugliest person I have ever sheen."

"And you," screamed the lady, "are the drunkest man I have ever seen!"

"Maybe," said the drunk, "but tomorrow I'll be sober."

****

Bourbon Baked Beans

4 cans (13 ounces each) baked beans
4 medium-sized oranges, sliced
1 medium-sized lemon, sliced
1 cup seedless raisins
1 cup molasses
1 cup ginger
½ cup Bourbon

Combine beans, oranges, lemon, raisins, molasses, and ginger in a shallow three-quart baking dish. Mix well together. Gradually add Bourbon and mix to blend. Bake in a slow 300° oven for about 40 minutes, or until thoroughly heated. Yields eight servings.

****

An American tourist, sitting in an English pub, was surprised to see a customer walk up to the bar, down a drink, pay for it, and, as he started to leave the tavern, walk up the wall, walk across the ceiling, walk down the other wall, and walk out the door. The startled tourist turned to the barmaid and said, "He's rather a peculiar fellow, isn't he?"

"He certainly is," she replied. "'E never says goodnight."

****

Green Beans with a Head on 'Em

3 packages (9 ounces each) frozen cut string beans
2 red onions, sliced
¼ cup cider vinegar
3 tablespoons Beer
⅔ cup salad oil
1 package blue cheese salad dressing mix
1 small head iceberg lettuce

Cook beans as directed on the package. Drain and cool. Toss with onion rings and chill. Combine vinegar, Beer, oil, and salad dressing mix. Beat until smooth. Line salad bowl with lettuce leaves. Mix green beans with the salad dressing. Spoon onto lettuce leaves and serve immediately. Yields ten servings.

****

Jack Carter told me about the drunk that fell three floors down an elevator shaft. When he regained consciousness, he yelled, "I said, up!"

****

Sherry Broccoli

1 package (1½ ounces) cheese sauce mix
½ cup milk
½ cup dry Sherry
4 toast slices
1 small can deviled ham
1 package (10 ounces) frozen broccoli, cooked and drained
Paprika, to taste

Empty cheese sauce mix into a saucepan. Stir in milk and Sherry. Bring to a boil stirring constantly. Let stand over hot water until ready to serve. Spread toast with deviled ham. Place broccoli on toast. Pour cheese sauce over each. Dust with paprika and serve immediately. Serves four.

****

"Is your husband a teetotaler?"
"He drinks nothing but pop, but pop will drink anything!"

****

Carrots Bourbonade

8 small carrots
2 tablespoons butter
2 tablespoons brown sugar
⅛ teaspoon salt
2 tablespoons Bourbon
1 teaspoon chopped fresh dill

Scrape carrots and slice in diagonal slices. Combine butter, sugar, and salt in a saucepan. Cook over low heat until butter melts, stirring occasionally. Add carrots and cook, covered, over low heat for 10 to 12 minutes or until tender. Add Bourbon and cook over low heat uncovered, for 1 minute. Sprinkle with dill and serve. Yields two servings.

****

Toast: Here's to good old Uncle Ben
      An astonishing man, I think.
      During his life he spilled more booze
      Than most people ever drink!

****

Braised Whiskey Onions

2 tablespoons olive oil
2 tablespoons melted butter
4 large onions, sliced about 2 inches thick
1 teaspoon salt
½ teaspoon finely ground black pepper
¼ cup beef broth
¼ cup Bourbon

Melt the oil and butter together in a heavy saucepan. Add
the onions and sear over a high flame for about 2 minutes.
Add salt, pepper, and broth and lower flame. Cover and
simmer for about 10 minutes. Add the Bourbon and allow
the sauce to reduce slightly. These onions go well with
lamb, beef, or chicken. Serves four.

****

One drunk to another: I've been dishpossessed. They're
repairing the gutter.

****

Brandied Potatoes

1 pound potatoes
½ cup Brandy
1 teaspoon salt
2 ounces butter

1 large onion, chopped
Salt to taste
½ teaspoon pepper
Chopped parsley

Peel potatoes. Cut into ½-inch slices. Place in a large frying pan or baking dish and pour Brandy over all. Cook over medium heat uncovered, until all liquid has been absorbed, turning once. Sprinkle with salt, add butter then sauté potatoes until golden brown on both sides. Add chopped onion halfway through the browning process; drain well. Serve seasoned with salt, pepper and topped generously with chopped parsley. Serves two or three.

****

My uncle saw a sign that read, "DRINK CANADA DRY." So he went up there!

****

Cups of Gold Potatoes Flambé

6 medium navel oranges
1½ cups mashed cooked yams or sweet potatoes
        (about 1 pound)
2 tablespoons melted butter
¼ teaspoon salt
½ cup Bourbon
Marshmallows studded with cloves

Cut oranges in half, crosswise. Section oranges and reserve. Remove and discard membrane from orange shells. Reserve orange shells. Combine yams, butter, salt, and ¼ cup of Bourbon. Blend well. Add orange sections and any juice. Mix lightly. Fill orange shells with potato mixture. Arrange in shallow baking dish. Top with clove-studded marshmallows. Bake at about 350° for about 20 minutes or until entirely heated. Arrange orange cups on flame-proof serving dish. Pour remaining ¼ cup of Bourbon on dish, around oranges. Ignite Bourbon. Serve immediately. Should serve about six.

****

Farmer: When my uncle died, he was so fulla corn likker, they had to shuck him before they could bury him.

****

Bavarian Kraut

1 slice bacon
¼ cup chopped onion
3½ cups undrained sauerkraut
½ teaspoon caraway seed
½ teaspoon juniper berries
⅛ teaspoon white pepper
1 medium apple, diced
½ cup Chablis wine
Knockwurst

Cut bacon into thin strips and sauté in a saucepan until lightly browned. Add onion and cook until barely crisp. Add sauerkraut, caraway seed, juniper berries, white pepper, apple, and wine. Simmer, uncovered for 20 minutes. Serve hot, with knockwurst. Yields four to six servings.

****

Fireman pulling drunk out of burning bed: You darned fool, that'll teach you not to smoke in bed!
Drunk: I wasn't smoking in bed. It was on fire when I lay down."

****

Tomatoes (Mel) Torme

6 large ripe tomatoes
1/3 cup olive oil
1 teaspoon salt
2 tablespoons Bourbon
1 tablespoon basil
1 tablespoon parsley
1 teaspoon grated lemon peel

Peel the tomatoes by piercing each with a fork, holding over a burner, and turning until skin is tight and shiny. Plunge in cold water. The skin will peel off easily. Slice thinly and arrange on a platter. Mix well together the rest of the ingredients. Sprinkle over the tomatoes and allow to stand for about 15 minutes before serving. Serves six to eight.

5

Desserts

****

One drunk was watching another drunk drinking. After every drink the second drunk would cry and then he'd drink some more.

"Washamatter, buddy?" inquired the first drunk. "Why are you so depressed?"

"Well," said the second drunk, "my wife ran away with my best friend, and I miss him!"

****

Kay Amsterdam's Bananas Aloha

4 bananas
Dash of cinnamon
4 tablespoons brown sugar
2 teaspoons lime juice

Juice from one-half orange
4 tablespoons butter
Grand Marnier to taste
Walnuts

Peel and slice bananas about one-quarter inch thick. Sprinkle with a dash of cinnamon, brown sugar, lime juice, and orange juice. Sauté in butter, turning occasionally. Pour Grand Marnier into mixture and serve hot with vanilla ice cream. Sprinkle with walnuts.

****

"Shcuse me, Offisher, where's Forth-seventh Street and Park Avenue?"
"You're standing on it."
"No wonder I couldn't find it!"

****

Strawberries Romanoff

1 pint vanilla ice cream
1 cup heavy cream
5 ounces Cointreau
2 quarts strawberries, chilled

Whip ice cream slightly. Whip heavy cream until stiff and fold into ice cream. Add Cointreau and blend. Crush one pint of the strawberries and mix with the whole berries. Combine ice cream mixture and berries and blend. Equally good with raspberries, blueberries, or fresh peaches. Serves six.

****

Two drunks were seated on one of those famous London double-decker buses. After a while one said to the other, "I'm going upstairs to get some fresh air." A few moments later he came flying down the stairs and said to his friend, "I ain't riding up there. It's too dangerous. There's no driver!"

****

Home-Style Ice Cream Cake

2 eight-inch round sponge cake layers
½ cup Blended Whiskey
1 pound glacéd fruit
½ cup pecan halves
½ pint each softened chocolate, pistachio,
**   strawberry, and vanilla ice cream**
Whipping cream

Cut sponge cake layers in half lengthwise to make four layers. Combine Whiskey and glacéd fruit in a saucepan. Cover and bring to boil. Remove from heat and stir in pecan halves. Place one sponge cake layer in an eight-inch spring-form pan. Spread with softened chocolate ice cream and top with ¾ cup of fruit-pecan mixture. Repeat layers with cake, pistachio ice cream, fruit-pecan mixture, cake, strawberry ice cream, fruit-pecan mixture, cake, vanilla ice cream, and fruit-pecan mixture. Freeze. Decorate with sweetened whipped cream before serving.

****

A Scotsman walked into a fancy bar, ordered a glass of beer, and put 50¢ down on the counter. "What's this?" asked the bartender. A glass of beer here is $2.00."

"Two dollars?" complained the Scot. "Every other place in town charges only 50¢."

"Did you happen to notice where you are?" said the bartender. "Just look at the paintings on these walls. They are worth over $500,000."

"Oh," said the Scot as he paid the two dollars and walked out. Next night he returned, put 50¢ on the bar, covered his eyes with his hands and said, "Gimmie a glass of beer, I saw the pictures yesterday!"

****

Pennsylvania Dutch Orange Cake

1¼ cups butter
2²/₃ cups sugar
2 tablespoons grated orange rind
2 tablespoons Curaçao Liqueur
5 eggs
3 cups sifted cake flour
3 teaspoons baking powder
¼ teaspoon salt
¾ cup orange juice
½ cup Bourbon

Cream 1 cup butter with 2 cups sugar until light and fluffy. Add orange rind and Curaçao and mix well. Add eggs, one at a time, beating well after each addition. Sift flour, baking powder, and salt together. Add alternately small portions of flour mixture then orange juice to the butter mixture, beating well after each addition. Turn into a greased and floured 10-inch tube pan. Bake in a 350° oven for one hour or until cake tests done.

Make a bourbon glaze for the cake by combining ¼ cup butter, ⅔ cup sugar, and the Bourbon. Heat until sugar has melted. Pour over the baked hot cake. Remove cake from pan when thoroughly cooled.

****

"I'm sorry sir," the stewardess explained to the intoxicated passenger. "Your ticket says 'Toronto, Canada' and this is a nonstop flight to Atlanta."

"Oh, my God," said the drunk, "have you told thish to the pilot?"

****

Diana Trask's Trifles

2 small sponge cakes, one-day-old
Strawberry jam
¼ cup Brandy, Sherry, or Port Wine
½ cup 7-Up
2 teaspoons butter
1 large tablespoon cornstarch

¼ **cup sugar**
2 eggs
1 cup milk
1 pint heavy cream
1 teaspoon sugar
½ **teaspoon vanilla**

Cut up sponge cake into slices. Spread with jam. Pour Brandy and 7-Up over sponge cake slices. Let stand till liquid is absorbed.

To make the custard melt the butter in a saucepan. Combine sugar and cornstarch and add to the hot butter. Beat eggs and slowly add. Gradually add milk until custard thickens. Pour over sponge cake slices and cool.

Whip the heavy cream and sweeten with sugar and vanilla. Top the cake and custard with the whipped cream. Keep chilled until ready to serve. Serves eight.

****

A drunk walked up to a parking meter, put a nickel in the slot, looked at the clock across the street, and said, "My god! I've losht forty pounds!"

****

Whiskey Cake

½ **cup butter**
1 **cup sugar**
3 **eggs**
1 **cup flour**
½ **teaspoon baking powder**
¼ **teaspoon salt**
½ **teaspoon nutmeg**
¼ **cup milk**
¼ **cup molasses**
¼ **teaspoon baking soda**
1 **pound seedless raisins**
2 **cups pecans**
¼ **cup Bourbon**

Cream the butter with the sugar. Beat the eggs and add. Mix flour, baking powder, salt, and nutmeg and add to the butter mixture. Add milk. Mix baking soda with the molasses and add to the butter mixture. Add raisins and Bourbon. Pour into a greased and floured loaf pan and bake at 300° for 2 hours. Whiskey Cake lasts indefinitely if kept wrapped in the refrigerator. It gets better if you stab it once in a while with an ice pick and inject a little whiskey with an eyedropper.

****

Toast

Here's to the gladness of her gladness
when she's glad;
Here's to the sadness of her sadness
when she's sad;
But the gladness of her gladness,
and the sadness of her sadness,
Don't compare with the madness
of her madness when she's mad.

****

Palatschinken or Crepes Loganberry

(Suggested by Giesele Gunther)

1 cup sifted flour
¼ cup sugar
¼ teaspoon salt
3 eggs, separated
½ cup milk
½ cup heavy cream
2 tablespoons melted butter
3 cups loganberries
Few drops vanilla extract
Few drops rum
1 cup granulated sugar, flavored with a vanilla
    bean for several days
1 to 2 ounces Kirsch, Eau-de-Vie de Poire,
    Rum, or Cognac

It is best to make this dish at the table, either over a flame with a French crepe pan, or in an electric frying pan.

Sift flour, sugar, and salt together. Beat egg yolks with rotary beater. Beat in milk, cream, and melted butter. Turn flour mixture into egg mixture and whip until batter is smooth. Beat egg whites until stiff and gently fold in. Grease a ten-inch skillet with a little butter and, when moderately hot, add vanilla extract and rum, then pour in enough batter to cover the bottom of the skillet with a thick layer. Cook over medium heat until pancake is golden brown on underside; turn. Across the middle line of the pancake, spread loganberries. They should warm through while the pancake browns. When cooked roll up with the loganberries inside. Sprinkle generously with the vanilla-flavored sugar. Douse with any or a combination of all of the above liquors and ignite. Serve immediately. Makes eight to ten crepes.

****

"Get away from my door, you miserable drunk! You're trying to get into the wrong house!"

"Itsh your fault, lady, you're looking out the wrong window!"

****

Chocolate Mousse Pie

4 eggs, separated
½ cup sugar
4 teaspoons instant coffee

1 tablespoon hot water
1 cup heavy cream
3 tablespoons Crème de Cacao
Graham cracker pie crust

Beat egg whites until stiff, then add the sugar. Dissolve the coffee in hot water and fold into the egg whites. In a second bowl, beat yolks until thick. In a third bowl whip cream and fold the Crème de Cacao into the cream. Fold egg yolks and whipped cream into the egg whites mixture. Pour into a graham cracker pie crust. Chill several hours in freezer until serving time.

****

Irate wife: You haven't been home since yesterday! Where were you?
Boozer: I sat up all night with a sick friend.
Irate wife: Who was it?
Boozer: I don't know, he was too sick to tell me!

****

Marcia Haber's
Tipsy Grasshopper Pie

25 chocolate wafers
4 or 5 tablespoons melted butter
25 marshmallows

²/₃ cup milk
3 ounces Crème de Menthe
1½ ounces of White Crème de Cacao
½ pint heavy cream

Crush chocolate cookies and reserve enough for a garnish. Combine with melted butter and press mixture into a pie dish. Freeze to set. Melt marshmallows and milk in a double boiler. Cool. Add Crème de Menthe and Crème de Cacao. Whip cream until very stiff and fold into the marshmallows and liqueur mixture. Pour into the frozen pie shell. Top with cookie crumbs. Freeze until a few minutes before serving.

****

"I know my husband came home drunk last night."
Her friend inquired, "What makes you think he was tight?"
"Because," said his wife, "as we were going to bed, he tried to take his pants off over his head."

****

Old English Mince Pie

2 cups prepared mincemeat
2 cups diced tart apples
1 tablespoon Brandy
Dough for a two-crust eight-inch pie
Hard sauce, vanilla-flavored

Mix mincemeat, apples, and Brandy. Line an eight-inch pie pan with pie dough. Fill with mincemeat mixture. Top with remaining pastry, cut to fit, and cut slits into the top. Bake at 400° for 35 minutes. Serve warm with a vanilla-flavored hard sauce.

****

"I just heard about the terrible party at Joe's house last night. They tell me it was a real orgy."

"Tsk, tsk."

"Everybody running around, blind drunk and nude. . ."

"Tsk, tsk."

"Somebody finally called the cops and they arrested everybody."

"My . . . my. Listen . . . can I ask you a question about that party?"

"What?"

"Was I there?"

****

Palm Springs Delight
(Suggested by Esta Wagner)

1 envelope unflavored gelatin
½ cup Bourbon
4 eggs, separated
½ cup firmly packed brown sugar
1½ tablespoons cornstarch
1½ cups milk

1½ **ounces unsweetened chocolate, melted**
½ **teaspoon vanilla**
1 **nine-inch baked pie crust**
¼ **teaspoon cream of tartar**
½ **cup granulated sugar**
½ **cup heavy cream, whipped**
Grated chocolate

Soften gelatin in ¼ cup of Bourbon. Beat egg yolks, slightly. Add brown sugar and cornstarch; beat until light and fluffy. Gradually stir in milk, and ¼ cup of Bourbon, and cook over hot water, stirring constantly. When thickened and smooth, remove from heat. Remove 1 cup of custard mixture and add melted chocolate and vanilla to it. Mix well. Cool slightly and pour into the pie shell. To the remaining custard mixture add the gelatin mixture and stir until gelatin dissolves. Cool slightly. Beat egg whites and cream of tartar until soft peaks form. Gradually add granulated sugar and continue beating until stiff and glossy. Fold egg whites into gelatin-custard mixture. Chill until firm. Spoon around edge of pie and sprinkle grated chocolate over all. Serve topped with whipped cream.

****

A hungry boozer walked into a Dairy Lunch, hailed the waiter, and said, "Gimmie two rotten eggs, some burnt toast, and a warm glass of beer. When the waiter asked, "Why?" the drunk said, "I got a tape worm and that's good enough for him!"

****

French Baked Applesauce

2½ pounds cooking apples, peeled, cored, and
    sliced ¼ inch thick
6 tablespoons butter
²/₃ cup sugar
½ cup Brandy
Milk
4 eggs
2 teaspoons vanilla extract
¼ teaspoon salt
1 cup sifted flour

Sauté the apples in 5 tablespoons of the butter until they are golden. They should be firm and not mushy. Sprinkle them with the sugar and pour the Brandy over them. Let sit for one-half hour, then drain off and measure the liquid. Add enough milk to make 2½ cups of liquid. Preheat the oven to 400°. In a blender combine the 2½ cups of liquid with eggs, vanilla extract, salt, and flour and blend for about 1 minute. Butter two Pyrex dishes with the remaining butter. Pour a thin layer of the batter in the blender into each one and place on an asbestos pad over very low heat until set. Divide the apples between the two dishes, and spread over the batter. Pour the remaining batter over the apples. Bake for 35 to 40 minutes or until the batter is cooked through but still moist and custardy. Reduce heat to 350° for the last 10 minutes if batter is getting too brown on top. Serves twelve.

****

A drunk was being bawled out by his wife. "And another thing, "she continued, "if you come home stinking drunk one more night, I swear you'll turn into a rat!" Next night he came home again, this time a little more stoned than usual. He called the butler over and whispered, "Lishen, Max, if you suddenly see me getting smaller and smaller, keep your eye on that cat!"

****

Booze on a Cloud

¾ **cup sugar**
1 envelope unflavored gelatin
3 eggs, separated
¾ **cup Bourbon**
½ **cup chopped walnuts**
1 cup heavy cream, whipped
Fresh strawberries

Combine 6 tablespoons of sugar and gelatin and mix well. Beat egg yolks slightly. Gradually add Bourbon, stirring constantly. (Adding the Bourbon too quickly tends to "cook" the egg yolks.) Add egg yolk mixture to the sugar and gelatin. Cook over hot but not boiling water, stirring constantly. Stir until mixture coats a metal spoon (about ten minutes). Beat egg whites until foamy. Gradually add remaining 6 tablespoons of sugar and continue beating until stiff and glossy. Fold in yolk mixture. Chill 20 minutes. Fold in walnuts and cream. Turn into a 4- or 5-cup mold. Chill until firm. Unmold. Serve garnished with strawberries. Serves six to eight.

****

"How did alcohol kill your uncle?"
"My aunt rubbed it on his back and he broke his neck trying to lick it off!"

****

Baked Carrot Rum Pudding

½ cup shortening
½ cup firmly packed brown sugar
2 well-beaten eggs
1 cup grated carrots
½ cup seedless raisins
½ cup Rum
1¼ cups sifted flour
1 teaspoon baking soda
½ teaspoon baking powder
½ teaspoon nutmeg
½ teaspoon cinnamon

Cream shortening and sugar together. Add eggs, carrots, raisins, and Rum. Mix well. Sift flour, baking soda, baking powder, nutmeg, and cinnamon together. Add flour mixture to Rum mixture and mix well. Turn into a greased, one-quart mold. Bake in a 350° oven for about 35 minutes or until pudding tests done. Cool about 15 minutes. Unmold and serve with Rum sauce. Serves six.

****

Lawyer: But if a man is on his hands and knees in the middle of the road, does that prove he's been drinking?
Policeman: No sir, it does not. But this guy was trying to roll up the white line!

****

Coffee Brandy Snowdrifts

2 envelopes unflavored gelatin
2 tablespoons Brandy
1 cup cold, strong coffee
¼ cup sugar
¼ cup half-and-half
2 cups crushed ice

Combine gelatin, brandy, and coffee in an electric blender. Cover and blend for 40 seconds. Add sugar and blend 10 seconds. Add half-and-half and crushed ice. Cover and blend for 1 minute, then let stand in blender for another minute. Pour into 6 individual parfait glasses. The mixture will firm up without refrigeration but, if you are in a hurry, refrigerate briefly. Serves six.

****

Lady of the house to drunken maid: "Lillian, did you put fresh water in the goldfish bowl?"
Maid Lillian: "No Ma'am. They didn't drink up what I gave 'em yesterday!"

****

Crema (Tony) Romano

2 cups heavy cream
Sugar to taste
Dash of lemon extract
1 pound creamed ricotta cheese
2 tablespoons instant coffee
1½ tablespoons confectioners' sugar
1½ ounces Kahlúa

Whip the heavy cream and sweeten with sugar and lemon extract. In an electric blender combine ricotta cheese, instant coffee, confectioners' sugar, 1 ounce of Kahlúa. Blend until very smooth. Slowly add whipped cream until thoroughly blended. Pour ½ ounce Kahlúa in the bottom of each dessert dish and fill with mixture. Top with a fruit sauce and a dash of whipped cream. Serves four.

****

A drunk was standing at the bar with a live lobster under his arm. The bartender asked, "Are you going to take the lobster home for dinner?"

"No," replied the drunk. "I took him home for dinner last night. Tonight I'm gonna take him to the movies!"

****

Lemon-Marsala Pudding

¾ **cup sugar**
2 tablespoons sifted flour
½ teaspoon cinnamon
½ teaspoon salt
2 whole eggs, plus 2 separated eggs
3 tablespoons Marsala Wine
1 lemon
1 cup milk

Blend together sugar, cinnamon, and salt. In another bowl
beat 2 eggs and 1 egg yolk with 3 tablespoons of Marsala
wine. Add juice and rind of 1 lemon. Add egg mixture to
the dry ingredients. Stir in 1 cup of milk. Fold in two
beaten egg whites. Pour into a buttered baking dish. Set
dish in a pan of hot water and bake in a moderate 350°
oven for 25 to 30 minutes. Cool. Serve chilled with a
brown sugar sauce.